Table of Contents

Table of Contents i
Author's Notes ii
Forward iii
Prologue iv
Chapter 1: Beginnings 1
Chapter 2: A Neuro-Hacker is Born 8
Chapter 3: Botanical Medicine 11
Chapter 4: On Mental Illness 14
Chapter 5: Buddy 17
Chapter 6: Beyond Mushrooms 20
Chapter 7: Fallacy of Suicide 25
Chapter 8: The Puzzle 31
Chapter 9: An Imperfect Storm - Creating BPD 33
Chapter 10: Meeting My Inner Child 36
Chapter 11: LOVE 38
Chapter 12: The Great Unhappening 40
Chapter 13: The Jeremy's Bodies 43
Chapter 14: Greta's Land 47
Chapter 15: Time Does Not Exist 49
Chapter 16: Integration 50
Chapter 17: And She Lived Happily-enough After 53
Appendix A: Postscript- Letters to different audience members 56

Author's Notes

This account is a mix of past journal entries, life tales and the author's commentary. For the ease of reading the *journal entries are in italics*, the commentary is in regular type, and the **trip account is in bold type**. I hope this will help the reader access the trip report with or without the contextual information.

To find out more about my current and upcoming projects go to:

AlteredStatesIntegration.com

Forward

If you are here, it's likely for one of two reasons: to heal or be healed. That's what we were told at my opening semester at Bastyr University. Likely, that applies to the reader (you) now, and more often than not, you fall into both categories.

When I wrote this trip account, I had the professional and researcher in mind. Please, please, please, if you have mental health issues, don't journey without support and a framework to guide you through the darkness. Even as you read this, safe journeys other me.

~Namaste.

Prologue

The author works as a traveling medical worker taking short-term contracts in hard to staff locations. This story takes place after an on the job conflict sends her career up in flames in the Summer of 2017. In an effort to self medicate with travel, she went to Oregon to see the solar eclipse where she met Buddy while hitchhiking. They became fast friends on their travels to Nevada for a festival where they were both working with the Zendo Project.

Upon returning to Texas, EJO had no job prospects on the horizon and decided to spend four weeks doing hurricane relief work near Corpus Christi. It was a tremulous time full of work and alcohol where she fell in love with a fellow volunteer, Caterpillar. As her career regained its momentum and beckoned her away, EJO tried chasing love to Austin, TX.

Work soon pulled her to travel to the gloomy Northwest, and the romance ended with an emotional bang. For the first time in a decade of travel, EJO was lost. Her emotions spiraled out of control, and she heeded advice to find a place to settle down and find grounding. Despite the history of heartbreak, Austin called her to make it home even if it's for a little while. This is her recent journey fighting Borderline Personality Disorder (BPD) using psychology and the plant medicine Iboga.

1
Beginnings

Morning 1 Post Iboga: The day I woke up.
There is so much love and gratitude coming to me; I now have a feeling of infinite love. Every time I feel this love, I wash it mentally over me. I consciously build it up to a higher frequency every time. I'm trying to keep the feeling from the drugs last as long as possible until it's a habit. Then I can maintain it infinitesimally...

I find endless joy in the realization that I unconsciously set up my experience months prior to obtaining the medicine and finalizing the space for my iboga journey. It is perhaps my Magnus opus or my 'great escape'. I realize now that I engineered a great protocol that can lend a scientific explanation to my evident success. The process is easily broken into three parts: the preparation, intervention, and integration.

Months before I knew that I would really become desperate enough to do iboga, I had re-enrolled myself in a DBT-informed psycho-educational class online (emotionallysensitive.com). It was an emotional skill-building workshop that Dialectical Behavioral Therapy (DBT) is known for without the support of a personal therapist. It was not my first entry point to the world of DBT.

At the time, I had met a very special someone named Caterpillar, sending my BPD (Borderline Personality Disorder) symptoms into full throttle. I had anxiety attacks with genuine physical responses for the first time in a decade. I wanted to be in therapy for support but couldn't get all the pieces together before my lover saw a dysphoric rage and cut off all ties with me. The emotional turmoil that followed was more than overwhelming thought and included a racing heart, cold chills with goosebumps, insomnia, and nausea. I could not stop the physical symptoms even as I tried to work the DBT skills.

November 9th, 2017
To the world: there are no second chances. I Fucked up, and I'll be paying for it until I die. I want to die, as soon I can get up the courage, I'm gone. Sure, it will cause pain, but they will get over me. It's my suffering I can't stand. Why should I hold on...

During this difficult time, my therapist suggested I write out a Trauma List including how those things made me feel. I'd never spoken at length about my childhood or journaled it in detail because 'it happened' and 'it was fucked.' It was the first time I'd actually written or admitted some of these things even to myself. It fell in line with a list I had started for my DBT class of Negative Self Messages & Limiting Beliefs.

-No one will ever love me if... I'm broken...honest... emotional.
-Anything I do is futile... no one loves me.
-I'm too much trouble to date.

-I'm only good enough to fuck.
-If I'm good, I won't be left. If I'm good I'll be loved.
-I will never feel love again.
-I'll never get this right.
-I have no control.
-I make a better friend than lover.
-I have no control over who stays in my life.
-If I have to ask, you don't love me.

I was trying hard to come up with the antidote for the beliefs, but my mind just chewed on them like a rubber bone in a dogs mouth. I told my therapist that I had made a list, but she never inquired and I needed her prompting to be transparent with these intimate details. True to my relationships, I didn't know how to ask her to visit this dark corner of my mind. It seemed like we often focused on how I judged things ultimately causing my emotional reactions, a dysphoric rage. It felt like she was asking me not to feel because it was the only way I knew to be.

I was digging deeper, and I was falling apart.

I decided, partially out of a desperate need for stability and partly out of a tiny spark of hope, to move to Austin instead of traveling to Central America for my usual winter of beaches, festivals, and volunteer work. I found a room to rent and decided to treat my recovery like a job. I woke up before 10 am and went to bed around midnight opting out of the all week party available in Austin. I concentrated on eating healthy and exercising. I only had four months rent money in savings with little extra since I had been saving for the total cost of living six months in Latin America not one of the priciest cities in the USA.

I wish I could say things got better, but they did not. I experienced depression that rarely spiraled up to the mania I loved to experience with my BPD. This coupled with the fact, and fear, that I could run into my ex-lover at any time made my life the only job I could handle.

January 10th, 2018
Sometimes, it's hard to reconcile the will to live with the desire to die. Even now I go through the motions of my life. I numbly showered before my doctor's appointment today. Wishing to gain the courage to end myself the whole time.

I even ask myself why I would even bother with any of the mundane things when today could be my last.
Could it be a simple lack of courage? Not enough courage to live this life of suffering and loss? Not enough courage to escape this bodily prison?

I thought moving here would help. I thought a change of pace and a stable home would help me pick myself back up. I thought I could feel different for a while.

But I can't. I can't even wake up in the morning without crying into my pillow for an hour while I dream of ending my life.

I've worked hard at going through the motions. I've gone to bed on time, woke to meditate and do yoga or run on most days. I fasted from alcohol and moderated my pot smoking to a few nights a week. Yet, I'm still here lying in bed wishing to die, or rather, wishing to end the cycle of suffering and numbness. I can't even dream of a world where I'm happy today.

About a month into my time in Austin, my therapist fired me after I told her I was disappointed with our therapy sessions. She made it clear that our phone appointments were NOT DBT even though I was taking online DBT skills classes. Too late, I understood her point that it could only be DTB-informed, but we had a whole fight about it first. She expected only to give me general talk therapy.

Her point was valid; I wasn't doing emotion journals, coaching calls, or BCAs. In my defense, I was playing the role of a client and hadn't asserted my expectations. This was what I was seeking, and I would have loved to incorporate as much of the classic therapy as my situation as a traveler would allow. Surprisingly, I took this new abandonment with little emotional recoil. It was of little loss as I had already grown meaningful relationships with others who could talk me through my emotional crises much of the time.

In actuality, being fired by my therapist felt extremely motivating after I got over the initial shock and pride of this BPD milestone. While I couldn't clearly see my needs to ask for them in therapy, from my client's side view, my therapist brain quickly unwound the truth that I needed to commit more time to the DBT and recovery. I got serious about doing the homework from my DBT psycho-educational group. I spent hours researching "what is rumination and how can I stop it?" I journaled all the thoughts in my head, questioned where they came from, and challenged their very existence. Recovering became an obsession.

The intensive journaling I was doing gave me a quiet place to admit my deepest secrets aloud. As the words flowed out day after day, some of the words were shocking as if written by a stranger.

March 4th, 2018:   DBT homework: Self Soothing - Week 5
Thanks to everyone who discussed the thumb sucking in Q&A for this class. I had a big epiphany with this class. Another reason people find it hard to self-soothe (Debbie maybe add it to your slide) is because people actively prevented or shamed self-soothing in the past.

When I was young, I would rub a velvet scrap on my face and/or suck my thumb. Both of these things were frequent topics of conversation between my mother/family and other family or adults. They also tried the bad tasting nail polish to make me stop. My brother, who emotionally tormented, me would pull my thumb out of my mouth at any opportunity. He also destroyed several version of the velvet scrap (it was once a skirt) by running it over with the lawnmower and another time by burning it.

I'm very touch-sensitive and buy lots of silk clothing. Recently I've been fighting high anxiety by taking a silk scarf to bed with me to rub on my face. I've been feeling a little pinprick of shame the whole time without realizing it.

I'm glad that I can now understand how all these things fit together so I can stop feeling uncomfortable with my need to soothe.

... and as I type this, I think about all the men I relied on for a soothing touch when I didn't really want their attention. I hope I can learn to be comfortable giving myself affection with touch.

2
A Neuro-Hacker is Born

During the fall of 2017, after Caterpillar broke my heart and rejected the existence of my emotion regulation difficulties (mental illness). I was working in Seattle all alone doing a tedious job for hours with plenty of time to listen to podcasts. I put my attention on studying BPD and complex/childhood PTSD for the first time since finding DBT the decade before while in college. The data from the last ten years of BPD and trauma research was more than I could have hoped for.

In particular, some studies examine the neurological dysregulation of BPD patients in an MRI machine. Normal brains stimulated by emotional distress show activity in both the amygdala and the prefrontal cortex indicating a balance between impulse and rational thinking. BPD patients who were triggered showed low or no prefrontal cortex activity (logic) and high amygdala activity (instinct) illustrating that control is not just a matter of will power.

I cried to hear about the study and relistened several times. Dysphoric Rages are one of the most frightening symptoms I've dealt with. It's happening, I see it happening, and there is nothing I can seem to do differently. Then after all the adrenaline wears off, it's hard to remember exactly how everything went down.

Surely there was a way to hot-wire those two parts of the brain into talking again. Nuerohacking was all the rage with fringe body experimenters, and I learned all I could as I worked.

Later, as I settled into my life in Austin, I joined Jamie Wheal's six week Flow Fundamentals class that challenged convention and preached neuroplasticity. I wanted to learn what lit up my brain and how I could trigger it. The classes gave me insight into my coping style via my flow style. I'm a 'hard charger' who seeks flow states in novel environments. All the traveling around the world kept me sane over the past eight years by grabbing my immediate attention over and over again. This is new; I feel better. Since I wasn't traveling now, I was forced to seek additional skills to manage my workflow and regulate my emotions. I was learning an expanded framework for experimentation.

February 2018: Flow fundamentals Rest and Recovery Homework
1. I access flow more often than I realize.
2. There are more different types of flow than I realized.
3. I'm a verbal processor, and while writing is slow for me, it works to sort my thoughts more efficiently.
4. Recovery (mental health and daily health) like enlightenment, is an action that is repeated daily. It is not a destination: it is a practice!

I began to see all learning as an opportunity for growth and a chance to add more skills to my coping toolbox. DO WHAT WORKS was my mantra. Too long had I held on to my puritan childhood bias about what was good and what was bad. How long had I rejected things that fell far outside science? If a weekend workshop on Tapping (EFT) could make me feel better for five days then great. I figured it was five more days to come up with the next solution or until something stuck.

Each day presented its own struggles, and I met them without bias. I would sink into depression one day and journal myself out of it the next. I was learning various types of meditation such as Box Breathing and mantras. Yet, I was still being held down by the weight of easily generated, unwelcome, suicidal ideation. It was a neurological grove worn deep.

3
Botanical Medicine

Sometime in January 2018, while I waited to join Jamie's class and after losing my therapist, I became desperate enough to order Iboga TA (total alkaloids) from the internet. Erowid.org seemed to point to a common internet source. Since I had only a single, three-month contract since returning from my Central American tour last year, the cost was an extravagant sum in the hundreds. A small fee compared to the $4000 price of the detox clinics in Mexico. I don't have an opiate addiction, but iboga has a few associated deaths warranting careful administration under medical supervision. I had already committed myself to throwing my entire wealth, a few thousand dollars, at beating this problem once and for all. Or die trying I thought. A definite possibility if you read anything about iboga on the web. It didn't matter; I couldn't imagine another 20 years with this level of mental suffering.

Iboga is traditionally delivered as a tea that is drunk over several hours between purges. Some traditions drive the substance in to the psyche with literal paddles to the head. My herbalist wisdom generally defers to traditional practices, so thankfully Africa was far from my current financial means. The opiate detox clinics prefer the more controllable, pure ibogaine, the known psychedelic substance from the iboga root. The third choice is the concentrated, total alkaloid (TA) extract that is the equivalent of dehydrated iboga root tea. I naturally gravitated to the latter preparation since it contains all the extra stuff scientists generally deny are important to herbal medicine. My belief that herbs in their whole form are better was reinforced by reports that Iboga TA extract is easier to ingest with less vomiting. Since my mind also equates less vomiting with more absorption, the choice was easy.

I was advised to take 2.7gm of iboga TA after several exchanges of emails. I was sent a final protocol and some cautionary remarks including fasting:

"The TA must be mixed with a sour based liquid like yogurt (2 tablespoons) or ginger tea should you have a sensitive stomach please do ingest something against anti-nausea or put the TA into capsules. First ingest 400mg TA, an hour later 500mg TA an hour after that 1 gram TA and an hour later the rest of your advised dosage.

As soon as you have ingested the first portion of the TA, one must go lie down in a very dark room and move as little as possible when under the influence of TA, everything around you becomes heightened, therefore any light may hurt your eyes, and the noises around you will sound much louder, therefore, please assure that it is very dark and as quiet as possible.

Vomiting might occur, therefore it is advisable to have a bucket beside you during the treatment should you have a very sensitive stomach, please do ingest something to prevent nausea. As long as you do not vomit within the first 1-1.5 hours after ingesting the TA, you will be fine."

4
On Mental Illness

If you're like most people, talking about mental illness probably makes you uncomfortable. Either because of a natural aversion to the reality that the brain can be sick or because you have a sick brain. It can be confusing to a healthy person that the brain could hijack so much thinking that undesirable traits emerge from rage to self-harm. It seems natural to deny the frightening reality that we are not our brains and they can revolt on us. Or in the case of BPD, they can be miswired or programmed beyond our logical control. It's pretty ridiculous that we believe in government brainwashing experiments but not environmental brain-wiring. Most likely, we look away so that we don't have to admit our fragility and the possibility of this mental prison.

The brain-sick individual feels all these fears too and speaking about them can seem terrifying. Self-preservation means not admitting to being the weakest in the herd. No one wants to be known as the sick girl. While I might need extra help from my friends, I don't want to be treated differently. I don't want it to be my identity or how my every move is perceived. I don't want to become someone who is unsafe to love because I have a suicide risk 200x that of the general population.

One of the harder parts from where I'm standing with my sick brain is drawing the line between identifying with a mental illness experience and not seeming to give myself over to it. Ignoring the diagnosis sets one up for failure while identifying with the diagnosis sets one up for a self-fulfilling prophecy.

I consider myself to be a pretender and a pretty good one at that. 95% of my life looks okay from the outside. In fact, when I talk about BPD, most people adamantly deny that I could possibly be like Winona Ryder from "Girl Interrupted". That is the problem with having high functioning BPD. I'm never quite sick enough for others to see because I'm busy covering up my emotions and maintaining life. Then when I lose the juggling act, all I can do is watch as my life shatters around me. Inevitably, people I care about scatter as I 'overreact.'

I specifically do not use the words Borderline Personality Disorder for fear of backlash or even more distance in my relationships. I talk about trauma and abuse because most have some level of compassion for these terms. I loathe the words "mental illness" but don't know anything else that can describe the sick brain experience.

I get on kicks where 'I'm not sick' is my mantra. High functioning means that I can pretend that I 'struggle occasionally'. People in my life can deny that my crying is just a little dramatic because I pull in the public emotions long before the turmoil subsides. I often feel like I'm trying to convince someone I'm sick and damning myself by doing so. Ya know, the over-identification with the disease is making it worse, so they might think.

So I close it all inside and pretend that I don't think about escaping this body several times a week. I look good because I hold a job, pay my bills, and otherwise 'function'. Moreover, I used to think that was good when compared with the much more outwardly visible drama of my late teens and early twenties. Even then I hid how deep the pain went; how often I fantasized about escape. My teenage best friend of 15 years read this manuscript and wrote back, "I had no idea". As an adult, I covered it better but still had days where I couldn't even feed myself or get out of the bed because of my sick brain.

5
Buddy

A desire to help people in a psychedelic crisis is a special trait. It was the first of many topics Buddy, and I bonded over when he picked me up hitching from the Oregon Eclipse Festival to Burning Man during the summer of 2017. We both had a strong connection to conscientious drug use and were headed to the desert festival to volunteer as peer counselors at the Zendo Project, gifting our time to the unwary tripper. We also had an unexpected bond in regards to BPD. Just a few months earlier he had ended a seven-year relationship with a woman with evident borderline traits. Much of our conversation revolved around my clinical introspection into BPD and his perspective into dating and loving a woman afflicted with it.

While we traveled together, we inevitably had to work through the negative side effects of our obvious attraction. We gave a high priority to communication and succeeded in expanding our bandwidth for distress and depth of loving capacities. Meeting Buddy is part of the reason I felt secure to fall in love with Caterpillar a few weeks later. I thought, wow, I got this. Or not.

Buddy held space for me during those anxious months where I would flip from love to insecurity in the breath of a text or call. We talked about healing and psychedelic possibilities. Neither of us thought they were a cure-all or a panacea.

When I arrived in Seattle for my temp job in November, I extracted a promise from Buddy to come up from Portland to see me. He had some of the Northwest's finest mushrooms and was eager to share them if they could teach me to ease my suffering. We decided to rent a beautiful AirBnB in the Cascade mountains. We selected the apartment based on its separateness from the host's home since my voice carries at any volume. Being in a pine forest near a lake was a soothing bonus.

The first day was spent cooking dinner and becoming re-acquainted with each other. As the second evening approached, I felt unsure of the wisdom of going into an altered state with the conversation focused on the darkness of my childhood. I was looking for something to push me in a specific direction in my life. I needed to know what my next life goal was, now that Central America felt like an old bandaid. I was less interested in examining old wounds.

October 27th, 2017
Frankly, I don't remember much about the most important part of the trip. We delayed all day in part because of the heaviness of the conversation. I also felt we had a conflict of goals for the session. Buddy wanted to go deep into the trauma, and I wanted to seek direction on my current dilemma on what to do with my life. We also were a bit off schedule by the time we ate dinner, so we didn't dose (on psilocybin) until 6 o'clock. We dosed together which took the pressure off me for where the trip might go. Buddy felt it first, and we decided to take more

because of my delayed reaction. Buddy thought they might have lost potency. I took a total of 4 capsules (2gm), and he took 3 (1.5gm). I don't remember much except crying my eyes out for an hour talking about my childhood while buddy held me and validated my experience:

'Someone should have comforted you.'
'It's not your fault; you were upset.'
'It's not okay to be picked on.'

And as I lay on my back, my eyes became deep pools of tears that cascaded into my ears. As we talked, he would hold me and say:

'I'm so proud of you.'
'You're so strong.'

I felt all those things from him, and I felt safe and secure in my emotions in a way I've always desired.
I hope that it sticks/stays. I hope my mind is a little reprogrammed.

And in a way, it did stick. I finally experienced the primary emotions of hurt that had been under all those layers of overwhelm. I had experienced the comfort that I had never had when I was bullied and harassed by my brother for all those years. Finally, it felt like it was normal to have hurt emotions when someone picked or teased at me. I no longer had to feel broken because being upset is normal when dealt with cruelty.

6
Beyond Mushrooms

Why I chose Iboga was as much out of healers intuition as science. I've known for some time that a deeper psychedelic experience could be therapeutic; once a decade ago a boyfriend suggested a ten strip of LSD to crack open my head. I'd never felt inclined to try that much LSD as the jittery feeling I'd had on one dose felt too much like a panic attack to be attractive. That, and I had a very real fear it could push me into psychosis after seeing my roommate lose his mind to a LSD induced psychotic break when I was 17.

I'd strayed away from psilocybin most of my adult life due to the stomach-wrenching effects I'd always experienced. (This is easily resolved by drinking something acidic, but that's another story). Besides, I had used both of those substances with good and minimal results. Taking more was not the answer.

There has been a lot of attention on Ayahuasca in recent years. I had met several people who have done it both here and abroad. I even had the opportunity myself to do it in Peru and then again in Panama at a psychedelic-spiritual festival. Ayahuasca is known as an energetically feminine plant teacher, and the amazing visuals might include a visit from a spirit guide. While it falls under the category of closed-eyes psychedelics (experienced in the psyche), it seemed too out of the body and too otherworldly for my needs. I wanted to change my brain.

Iboga or ibogaine when it's called by its primary constituent is also a closed-eyed psychedelic experience. Recent attention has focused on ibogaine as a panacea for opiate addiction. There seems to be a biochemical clearing of the addiction cycle for opiates. Less is known about the more mysterious addictive urge quenching properties for nearly any chemical substance. After receiving a flood dose, patients report no cravings and a new perspective on how that substance played into their life of suffering. Iboga presents hallucinations that are more like a life review with the added benefit of a third person perspective that facilitates deeper understanding.

Since my problems seemed to stem from the conditioning of my childhood, a drug that revisited those years was appealing, if a bit frightening. I had questions about the majority of my younger years that were un-rememberable. Iboga is also said to be of the masculine energy, and my emotional dysregulation could be seen an energetic imbalance toward the feminine, so it appealed to me.

My trip sitter was more of a volunteer. In mid-February 2018, when I told Buddy that the iboga TA I'd ordered off the internet had come in the mail, it was the first he knew of my intention to take it beyond a passing interest. I was only partially into telling him about the overly packaged, mislabeled envelope when he interrupted, "I want to be there when you take it." I was relieved

I didn't have to work up the nerve to ask or convince him to fly across the country for me. This was a big ask. I was scared but committed to making it to the other side of suffering and Buddy was my support. He even assigned homework while arrangements were made.

March 12th, 2018:   3 days before Iboga
Writing prompt: target behaviors – blockages – things are not serving me - intentions – shadows?
Doing iboga is no easy thing to be sure. It is not something I approach lightly. In the time it took to acquire and arrange a sitter, things have changed, or rather, the energy has shifted. The energetic potential for deep depression and emotional crisis lies in wait as it ever does.

When I decided to seek iboga, the act was more akin to being in a dungeon and throwing oneself down the latrine shoot in hopes of escaping into the moat/river on the outside, that is, if there was even an outside. Then at the same time, knowing that if I drowned, the end would be welcomed.

I still feel that, as a distant urge, but it's not what drives me now. The thought of crisis returning does propel me into caring about the future not yet written.

I am at this date, of sober emotion making the decision to crack open my soul. I've worked on healing my body with exercise and diet and supplements. It brought me the level of strength to endure but has never changed the pain. I work to retrain my thinking with DBT, meditation, and yoga. It showed me how to moderate the frequency and duration of the crisis from time to time. The moments in between are so much richer because of the work. I have shed skin and carved off chunks of the rotting exterior. Still, there's a deeper source that urges me beyond reason and into darker spaces. One moment of inattention and a bad day becomes my last day. I'm so tired of feeling everything all at once.

I chose iboga because of all the plant teachers; he is known to deal in this plane and this lifetime. The distress that I feel is one I've always known. Even the best childhood memory is overshadowed by an all present "upsetness", crankiness, moodiness. I've begun to unwind the strings that connect me to my past in a more concrete way. It goes beyond my brother merely picking on me or my dad not being around or my mom not being emotionally stable. It's so much more complex.

For starters, I'm asking this plant teacher to buy me time and save me time. If I can learn/make connections regarding my past that will speed up the trauma healing process, maybe I can meet emotional stability sooner — even an energetic boost to keep me away from suicide just a little longer. Preferably, if you will, so I can catch my breath while I do the hard emotional work. At best, I hope the medicine can heal the physical pathways of the mind and open up possibilities I've never had. Can a plant heal the broken neurological connections of my youth?

I have questions, but they are much less important to me:
–Why can't I finish anything?
–Was I sexually abused?
–Why do I feel like it's all my fault?
–Why do I have such a strong desire/need to be right?

Thursday, March 15th, 2018: Iboga day
Well, it seems today is the day. Buddy is here and is in the process of taking control of the moment. I watched as he carefully stuffed the capsules with the iboga TA and weighed them out. He read my journal entry and asked poignant questions. I realize the risk he is taking and see it as a necessary challenge in his growth as a healer. These are the risks of a modern shaman.

7
Fallacy of Suicide

Death Scene
As I took the last pill, I was nervous. I tried to play it off, and maybe that worked. Buddy seemed like he was slightly worried. I felt a bit queasy. I wasn't feeling anything by the time I took the second dose. In fact, I was relaxing while sitting on the bed and talking with Buddy, probably because I was feeling nothing. By the time I took the third dose, I was feeling the edge of something, suddenly I was worried. I knew it was now or never. I would die or be healed. I took the last pill without being able to finish my yogurt. As I handed Buddy the yogurt, I felt physically less steady and I thought "my god girl what have you done." I went to the potty as I knew it would be the last chance for a while.

When I came back, I snuggled down under the covers with my eyes closed and things began to pop up in my mind's eye like little incomplete movies — a flash of two puppies. My heart was beating hard, and I had to check my Fitbit several times to make sure I was ok. Faces were swirling around me: mommy, my sister, my brother Jeremy, I saw the front of the Knowlton church. My heart was beating a mile a minute, or so I thought. I checked my Fitbit. I was hot, and everything around me turned red. I was petrified with fear because I knew I was dying. I saw an ambulance and paramedics. I saw my mom crying, and a man in white beckoned me to come. I was scared and fighting to live and yet trying to stay calm and accept the end if that's what was happening. I felt a shudder of remorse for not saying goodbye. I never even left a note to say I love you to anyone. No one but Buddy even knew I was there.

My conscious self would sharply inhale deeply as if remembering to breathe. I was grounding into my body with breath. I started box breathing several times instinctively. Panic was washing over me, but I was breathing in its waves.

Death was there in his shapeless robes. He told me it didn't matter what I pleaded; it was my time. I was so scared, scared as I've ever been of dying. Scared of what was next. I was begging death not to take me. He reminded me of all the times I wanted to die. All those desperate times when I had asked him to come for me. I was on my hands and knees clawing with my will at this new, pending reality. I was not done, I can't go. It felt futile…

On a particularly difficult day in February before my Iboga experience, I was reminded of a man I had been trying to forget for months. The grieving process was long and hard because he was a particularly nice guy, the kind you bring home to mother. Caterpillar was what drew me to this city initially and I'd worked hard to forget I could run into him at any moment.

A friend had mailed me a package of things I had left at her house while passing through on my drive cross country in the fall of 2017. It was a few items of sentimental and monetary value that she had promised to send me months before. I'd initially been excited when she texted that she had just sent them through the post office. Days later when the package didn't arrive, I realized with a panic, she had my ex-lovers address, and the downward spiral took hold.

February 2nd, 2018
This is where it gets critical. This is where it gets real.

Last night I realized Gaia had sent the package of the things I left in Kansas last Oct. They were to arrive on Saturday per the tracking number. I looked back through my correspondence with her and saw only one address, Caterpillar's! I feel the symptoms of stomach clenching, chills, and hearing my own heartbeat. I work to not let my thoughts go down a rabbit hole. I arranged to have someone pick it up. I felt the physical effects all night. Should not have had caffeine at the Tea & Flow Jam event! I did well yesterday... now not so much. I cry as I write this...

I journaled the Inner Critic's message:

-*I'll never feel ok about Caterpillar. I said his name out loud and GOOSEBUMPS!*
-*I should be alone.*
-*I only love him.*

And I kept writing

I'm trying to feel grateful for him and this moment to practice. The thought makes me cry like running in the rain. Pain and pushing on despite. Always pushing on because there is no safety net.

There are moments where I want to yell at him and hurt him. Show him he's wrong. To take away his "holiness". In the same moment, I want him to take me back. Some moments he's a monster, others a scared boy.

I imagine seeing him with someone else, and my heart aches(literally) and tears well up in my eyes.

I think back to his letter, and I feel defeated at the idea that I should be able to STOP having 'dysphoric rages'. It seems similar to my mom saying that I need to stop picking at this old wound. It means that somehow, I have control of when I feel very out of control. That I should be able to do it alone. That I'm lazy or lacking for not being able to overcome these things. I've tried so hard to be in control; it eats at me that I can't stop. It's what's been driving me to suicide.

And there it was so neat and uncomplicated.

It's a final solution. In the Bible, they suggest that if a hand causes you to sin, cut it off. If a tongue causes you to sin, cut it out.

Should I truly take this route?

I cannot, for all the trying I do, hold my tongue when I'm at a high state of arousal, so suicide is the only solution that I know will work to prevent me from hurting those I love most.

I still revel at the simplicity of it all. 25% of the time the physical and emotional pain were too much to bear, and I desired relief. 30% of the time, I'm desperately trying to punish myself for my transgressions against those I love. 45% of the time, it's both.

Finding this gem of psychological truth was not a cure by any means. My thoughts still had the quick tendency to jump down the rabbit hole and straight to the images of suicide. I could rationalize the fallacy and even went back to re-read the journal entry a few times. In the days following this revelation, there were days when I just laid there thinking of death.

...At some point, I surrendered into tears. Lying still, feeling myself start to leave my body, I saw images of crosses and myself, so I started to reflexively pray to Jesus as I've felt an impulse to do before in dire situations. But I stopped myself and I refused because I knew God is more. I felt more surrender. Surrender to an unknown all loving source. I felt reassured that I should let go of those illusions of the afterlife. I was drifting to the beyond; death was waiting patiently.

Then I saw a vision of Buddy crying. I was gone, and he was crushed with grief. He felt he had let me down; he had let me kill myself right in front of him. I knew I couldn't leave him to

hold that burden. What would happen to him if I died? I could accept death, but not today, not in this way… I may have opened my eyes at this point. I feel like I looked at Buddy or touch him. There's so much more love between us. He was my tether. I had made a promise, written in pen on paper, not to leave the space during our experience.

What I seem to have sorted out about death at that moment shifted my entire view of the world. Most importantly, I don't want to die. Suicide has been programmed as a punishment as much as an escape. I'm scared of dying. I'm not ready, and it's normal to be afraid of the unknown. Cherish every moment and have continued gratitude for the Now.

Secondly, I can also surrender to the fear. I can look into the infinite abyss of the unknown and be at peace. This happens literally every day as change scatters the future I once longed for. I don't know what thoughts will pop into my mind, but I doubt I will ever dance with suicide again. Skills will keep me sane. I'm learning to feel my emotions instead of hiding from them, no matter how strong they are.

8
The Puzzle

After thoughts of Buddy brought me back from dying, the visions were coming really fast. Individual scenes were playing out so fast, it was like each scene was playing on a page in a flip book. The pages of the book were being flipped rather fast, and it was all unintelligible. Over time, the flipping pages came less quickly, and the scene became slower and slower eventually separating out and becoming distinguishable. Each scene looked to be in its own container almost like a Steampunk shadow box.

As I viewed these boxes, I would be sucked into a scene and become part of it. They were all memories, hurtful memories. I was unable to affect the scene, only play out my part. Then I would be thrown out of the memory and boxes would shift as if on tracks like a Rubix cube. Creaking and groaning as a new one was brought front and center.

Curiously, the characters in the memories were all the wrong players, although it didn't seem to change the memory or make me confused. (I made no meaning of the bodily substitutions). There were dozens or hundreds of the scenes; I couldn't tell. I was stuck in a loop with them. Over and over I was drawn in and reliving the memories. It became obvious that the same scenes were playing over and over again. This must have gone on for some time.

At this point, I tried to explain to Buddy that it seemed to be a puzzle, and I couldn't figure out how to solve it. I needed to figure out how to make it stop repeating. I equated it to a time loop as represented by TV in Star Trek or Buffy the Vampire Slayer. They have an episode where the main character keeps repeating the same scene (many times with a disastrous end) until the right changes were made. Only I couldn't figure out how to make any changes.

I tried to speak with Buddy, which took quite an effort. Thankfully I made this intention before the trip started because it took a lot of willpower. I tried to tell him about the boxes. I even tried to tell him some of the scenes but couldn't completely tell him a memory before it was lost or overwhelmed by the next moment.

I had a sense of seeking why the puzzle was broken. Somewhere, underneath all the boxes, I found a place with some gears and a crank that was broken. Or maybe it was a piece of wood jammed into the cogs. The wooden part had been clawed or scratched at down to a nub. I knew this was my Stuck Spot. There were wood shavings, and sawdust pilled at its base. Someone had tried to make it move with desperation.

9
An Imperfect Storm - Creating BPD

Borderline Personality Disorder and other personality disorders are a classic example of an imbalance of scarcity and abundance. Growing up with a shortage of money, love, coping skills, security, companionship, or attention is not in and of itself what causes personality dysfunctions. It's the multiplicity of the factors. Two major factors such as poor coping skills and sexual abuse will create PTSD. But far overlooked is the child who has dozens of little risk factors. Perhaps a child like me.

I grew up in a relatively lucky situation. While my parents were separated when I was two and divorced by age eight, neither one had addiction problems, neither even smoked or drank. I grew up on an old farmstead with an abundance of outdoor activities, and we ruled the forest. My father was a seasonal worker at a ski resort in the nearby Poconos, so I had the privilege of learning to ski growing up.

I knew from a comparison to school mates that we were poor, but it wasn't until I was a young adult that I realized how poor we really were. To this day my mom or siblings will play it down, although my mom does say things when she's upset with my dad that might be closer to the truth. What really mattered was the sense of scarcity I grew up with. Every bill presented a new problem and a time of stress before it was resolved. While the cupboards were never empty because at least there was flour and oatmeal, there were rarely extra which my mom passed off as puritan frugality. I remember more than one box of food was found at our doorstep around the holidays. Anonymous checks found their way to our mailbox right after cars broke down or electricity was to be shut off.

My mom didn't handle her emotions well and was often yelling at my dad or us or crying to whoever would listen. She seemed to handle overt emergencies well, which is a trait we share. If the car broke down, she might cry for a minute but then would get right to work banging at the engine or flagging down help. She never beat us or even really hit us. She did lose her temper quite a bit hitting my brother and second sister. I very rarely got punished because I rarely did the things that got you spanked or your mouth washed out. My biggest crime was screaming and being upset by 'seemingly, nothing.'

I was initially a loving child and would hug anyone who let me close. This emotional empathy made me especially vulnerable to the teasing of my classmates for wearing 4th hand clothes. To top it off, everyone in the neighborhood picked on me too. My worst tormentor by far was my brother. While some of it was poignantly cruel, most of it was a constant action of bothering me by poking, name calling, and being in my space. He would antagonize, I would yell, then my mom would get involved, and we would both be in trouble. My childhood mantra came in a crying voice, 'it's not fair' and would be reflected back to me by my siblings when their own tolerance for screaming was used up.

I learned two very important maladaptive behaviors from this: 1 my feelings don't matter or are inappropriate for the situation and 2 I had to be even louder to be heard. In other words, I shouldn't feel like this, and the only way to get taken seriously was to explode. Never did anyone teach me how to be upset and get over it or how to have healthy boundaries. I was screaming inside my whole life and what people saw on the outside couldn't compare to the misery I felt.

Modern science adds a few more clues about creating BPD. Empathetic children tend to also be sensitive to the external and internal environment. So while some may tolerate a cold, economically heated house, others of us feel it like a painful emotion. Additionally, the disease of poverty kept me struggling monthly with an ear, nose and throat infections. If feeling cranky from ear pain or medications wasn't enough, I was plagued by nightmares likely from the antibiotics I took for nearly six years. I often had lucid terrors of snakes or spiders in my bed. It's no wonder I wet the bed through my childhood and shamefully hid it for fear of ridicule.

10
Meeting My Inner Child

For a while I was back at the scenes – shadowboxes getting sucked in over and over again. Finding the Stuck Spot didn't seem to have changed my ability to interact with the shadowboxes. It seemed as if I would be in this endless cycle forever.

While pondering the puzzle more, my mind wiggled down into a small gap between two of the boxes. Suddenly, it was if I was ripping space and time. Light shone through the tear. Then I came through the crack into a white space.

A girl was kneeling on the floor weeping into her hands. She is wearing a blue dress and had long black hair with bangs. I knew immediately that she was my inner child. Her overwhelming emotions could be felt coming off of her like waves on the ocean.

She looked up at me with red eyes and a sad smile. I realize instantly how I had been hurting her over and over and over again by threatening suicide. I was constantly pushing her instead of comforting her. And every time I wish to die, I was abandoning her. I thought of my past anger at her for crying so loudly. It dissolved into compassion; she was just a child and needed me.

"Hi, I'm Greta" she had stopped crying.
Me, "I'm sorry Greta. I'll never leave you again."
Greta, "I'm sorry I cried so much. I was so scared."
Me, "will you forgive me Greta?"
As we embraced, she said with a smile "of course I will..."
"...I already have" we said together ending in laughter. Because she is me and this is my way and philosophy to forgive first and always. I've worked hard to forgive everyone because I need so much forgiveness from the world.

I am filled with the most amazing love. Pure love. The little bell rings. It's like a signal in a video game telling the player the level has been completed.

Ding!

11
LOVE

In the moment of the embrace with Greta, there was a pinnacle moment of forgiveness from both sides. My sentient self forgiving my child self for screaming in terror at all she was ill prepared to endure. And me as my child self forgiving my adult self for trying to punish her for crying.

In that moment, I experienced the most infinite and pure love I have ever known. Love for myself, love for Greta, love for all moments, and all things. It was a sound, a feeling, and a sensation.

When I pulled back from that seemingly endless hug and there was a cosmic "tattoo" in the divet between my clavicle and my shoulder. It was an infinite white space with the word LOVE projecting out of it. The space hummed with the resonance of Om. And now when I think of the space or read the word "love", it is sung not spoken. When I remember this, I can still sense the cosmic tattoo under all the layers of this reality.

Ding!

Greta gave me a key. This key looked like a steampunk hand clenched in a fist except the pinky finger was sticking out. The finger was long and narrow and terminated in a skeleton key. I knew immediately that it went to the Stuck Place and traveled back there. (I never thought to ask before this moment why didn't she use it herself. Wasn't she strong enough? Or maybe our love manifested it to her.)

While I don't have a specific memory of the journey back, I imagine I had to travel back through the place with the boxes. Maybe I was delayed by being drawn into more scenes. Then I navigated dimensions to return to that gear room. It was exactly as I left it: Saul dust, cobwebs, stillness. I press the key deep into the top of the gearbox; things began to creek and groan and click and move.

Ding!

12
The Great Unhappening

The gear room is down, around, and under many layers of the shadow boxes. The place looks like the control room under a drawbridge. It was quiet in here as opposed to the groaning and clicking upstairs where the boxes danced in an endless loop. Dust and cobwebs show no one had been here in a long time. In what appears to be a switch box, a wooden rod/handle protruded from the top. It has been clawed into a nub. I didn't realize it until weeks after the experience, that the wood shavings at the stuck spot were from Greta desperately crying, trying to make it move. She was trying to "get out".

I withdrew the key made of the hand. I took it and fitted it down into the box and turned it. Time stopped. Above me, a rift opened into another dimension. A voice boom, "don't worry lady you've got a ticket to heaven."

For a moment, my mind went to a place past the shadow boxes. I saw a kiosk decorated like an 1800s Circus box at the beginning of the a ride. A Gold ticket popped out of the top.

Ding!

A hand reached down out of the tear. It was Maglifinence. I hand him up the key, the handle from the Stuck Spot, and the word "Love" from my chest. He handed them back combined as a beautiful wand. The key was the tip of the wand, the word was the butt of the handle, and the Stuck Spot was the handle, only there were flowering vines wrapped around it.

Ding!

When I left the gear room, I ran through that world lightly, knowing I had solved the puzzle. I passed the ticket kiosk leaving the ticket there, having no worries it would be there for me later. I got back to the boxes; they were running more smoothly. I was immediately caught and drawn into one memory after another. It was all different this time.

Immediately I could see my memories as if viewed by all sides. I could see past my child's filters and hurt. Now I could change the memories or at least as far as my responses were involved. I actively engaged in my DBT training, and then with a rush, I would be thrown out of the memory. The box would shrink down in size and pops out of existence. Each one followed by that distinctive Ding!

I had to go through all memories in the shadow boxes. I untwisted so many frayed and loose ends. It was like I theoretically went through all the things in my life and applied all the skills I'd gathered in my classes and therapy. When I had initially been drawn into the shadow boxes, they were not emotionally comfortable memories to visit. After the Unhappening, those memories lost their charge. Even now, I can think about the past without being overwhelmed by the emotion of that day or the endless despair that always connected those memories to the infinite suffering.

I could feel my neurons growing. They were unwinding from their past tangles and forming a new, more efficient network. The nueroplasticity was perceivable just like when I'm learning flow arts or studying a new language. I knew I could learn anything and actively choose new ways of being.

After the Unhappenings, I opened my eyes, or tried to in the blinding candlelight, and told Buddy I was done. I had solved the puzzle. I had a ticket to heaven. He gently suggested that maybe I should go back and there might be more to discover.

13
The Jeremy's Bodies

When I re-entered my mind, I was transported to a shapeless dimension where I approached three figures in the mist. They were vistas of my brother Jeremy.

One was him at around eight years old when I think we were still playmates. His face was round with youth, and he was smiling under black mopey bangs.

Lying in front of him was his lifeless body as it looks now. Beard and belly he grew as he aged into his thirties. He looked to be asleep, but I knew he was dead.

The last figure stood at his foot and was a leaner, perhaps younger version of his adult body. However, it was impossible to tell because his face was distorted and scarred like that of a demon. I knew this was not really my brother but the spirit that had tortured me all those years. I knew it was responsible for killing the prone figure of my brother. It had taken all the love and joy my brother could have given the world.

As I approached, I had a bag in my hand, and I reached up to smother the ugly faced Jeremy. I put the bag over his head and smothered him down with force I didn't know I possessed. The body broke into pieces. I put the broken parts with the dead,

actual Jeremy in a coffin. Somehow that made him whole, or it made his energy whole again.

Ding!

"What does that even mean?" I asked myself when I listened to the recording. Initially, I didn't remember this part of my trip. Confusion gave way to a wave of revulsion and resistance as the memory replayed. It was all so violent. For all of my past emotional volatility, I had never dream of committing such an act of violence against my brother.

I still loved my brother for all this constant pestering and acting out. As we aged, his attention became more abusive until I became violent in response, throwing butter knives at him or hitting. However, I was always holding back because I didn't want to hurt him, I just wanted him to stop.

I saw the hurt and rejection my brother felt as our parent's divorce tore our family apart. Needing and desiring love and attention only to get crumbs and broken promises can lead to deep resentment. I was empathetic to his plight and even cried if he was punished too harshly for his crimes.

I've always known that the people around me where doing the best that they could. Even as a child, I knew my mom was at her limit, hanging on a prayer. She didn't know what more to do about my brother's constant tormenting of me. At times, I felt like felt like my upset emotions were at fault as the whole family grew weary of my whining.

Empathy holds a burden that often feels like a responsibility. I see, I feel, I understand, therefore I should be able to do something about this. I was empathetic to everyone's situation yet unable to hold compassion for my own. I didn't see the inconsistency between accepting other people's poor behavior while feeling guilty for my own.

There was one last fight between us before I moved with my mom out-of-state and he opted to move to my dad's. I really fought back, kicking and biting until we were on the floor. I was done being the whipping boy for his anger. I didn't win that day; there was no winning. The ferocity surprised him though, and he gave me a wide berth until we moved several months later. That fight, that move, and that summer were very pivotal in my life.

I saw him rarely after we moved apart as teenagers. His presence manifested in Freudian ways in the men I met and dated. When I started traveling for work, I made attempts to visit a few times. He'd go on and on about himself and how life had wronged him. When he did ask me a question about my life, it was in an inflammatory tone or context. I wanted so badly for my big brother to hang out with me the way we had when we were little but we shared little in common, anymore.

What did I let go of during that grotesque scene with my brother? Frankly, I don't know. I just know that the brother that I loved is gone. It's unfortunate that not everybody changes at the same rate or intensity. I never imagined that I would have to make the choice between being a healthy individual and letting go of my desire for deeper family relationships. True to my compassion, I don't blame them; I just recognize the need to protect my own emotional stability when I've strived so hard to gain it.

Ultimately, it is less important why I let go and more important that I did.

14
Greta's Land

There was once an evil queen.... After solving the puzzle and unhappening all the shadow boxes, I returned to Greta with the key-wand. Greta then returned to her nest in the hidden corner of the Jurassic greenhouse that sat below the Cosmic Castle. She was tired and could finally rest. I didn't bother her there for some time thinking she would come find me.

Later, she would tell me she was still scared of the evil queen. We immediately went to nab the queen and stuff her into a cell in the dungeon. After the queen was gone, we spent long hours playing together in her realm. We reveled in freedom and love.

One day, while we flew around the castle as wispy wraiths, we came to two parallel, open vents. The air was rushing out at us like a river of air. A glimmer of light at the other end was visible in the distance. We paused with our ethereal bodies fluttering in the rush of air. As I looked over at Greta and laughed nervously, she said "it's OK, I get scared sometimes too". I was at awe at her bravery. So much strength for one so young. Greta assured me that she was with me and we rushed into the vents and adventure.

Ding!

I spent lifetimes playing with Greta. Towards the end of the trip, she no longer came when I called. It was distressing at first, and I kept asking Calista (Greta's doll and ironically Buddy's ex) where she went. My mind often went to her little nest to find her gone. Much later I realize she wasn't gone but integrated into myself; she was happy and safe at last.

June 19th, 2018: Facebook DBT Group Post - Can BPD be cured? Perhaps the confusion comes in because to be cured, "restored to health" means we were healthy in the first place. Most, if not all of us, experienced childhood trauma and may not remember/know what healthy feels like.

Healthy emotional balance doesn't look or feel like bliss. It doesn't look like not messing up or not having bad days. It looks like making mistakes and not making it out to be a catastrophe. Some days you might say the wrong thing, then have to feel humbled when apologizing. Healthy is not being comfortable all the time. It feels like mindfulness as you self-soothe or write out a DEAR MAN letter. Healthy is the little knowing Half Smile as you see your mind wander and bring it back to the task at hand. Healthy comes from all the little DBT ways I care for myself and others...

15
Time Does Not Exist

Time felt infinite there in that cosmic space. I could relax because I had all the time in the universe to do everything. I could travel to distant galaxies and into different dimensions. At one point, Buddy woke from a nap. I told him about my superpowers of telepathy and flying and time travel. Things were different when I close my eyes. "I've been alive for millions of years in there. I could go to a realm and meditate for 1 million years and return in a blink of an eye."

I close my eyes flew through space and time to a mountaintop and started to count my breaths, one... Two... Three... Four... Five... Six.... And onward. I was there forever before I came back to open my eyes and look at Buddy. "See I just meditated for 1 million years just like that." In reality, I came back way too soon. But I did feel like I left a little Buddha avatar sitting there doing my dirty work. I checked on him from time to time to see how dutifully he was toiling away as they sentenced him to an eternity of meditation. If I meditate now, I can still access him... 205035... 205036...

16
Integration

Integration is the process in which we take the ineffable and make it effable. We utter it in a language we understand. Altered states of consciousness change us in ways that we cannot explain to ourselves or others. In some way, we can never undo what was done, and generally, feel some sort of responsibility to act on this new knowledge or way of being. There is a desire to make ourselves better and therefore the world.

Full integration takes time and attention. It is easy to enter an altered state and brush it off as a simple dream state the next day for the most resistant minds. Recreational use can be flawed in that the individual may not have the skills alone to retain the insight from the trip or to manifest those lessons into life actions.

So how am I integrating? Well, you're reading this note I wrote to myself, so I would not forget. I've read it many times to edit it and recounted the tale to many intrigued friends. It's helping me keep the memory alive and real.

I remember feeling afraid while I was tripping, that I would forget everything and slip back into the shell of my own mind after being awakened the next day. I had gone into the experience with a beginner's mind and a desire for Buddy and I to learn as much as we could from our separate perspectives. This desire was how I was able to reach out through the fog to give him little clues into the Puzzle.

On the second evening of the trip, while I was drawing a picture of some of the events of the Puzzle, Buddy told me something he had learned from the Ibogaine clinic nurse: I might not remember much of the trip once I came down. It's a lot of the reason he recorded and asked questions and clarified my experience the whole 36 hours.

I might not remember! It was hard to fathom since it all seemed so real and clear to me at that moment. It also brought a bit of concern because how could I come so far and have it all taken away. Would I loose details? Would I lose this feeling of love? Would it be like amnesia of this new self that I was experiencing?

Buddy encouraged me to write, but the connection between my pen and brain seemed jet-lagged. I did manage a drawing that appeared to perfectly represent my experience. After dinner, he listened and recorded as I explained the whole peak experience from my drawing. We were already recording almost constantly on the second day. This gave me some sense of security.

That night we decided to put the mattress on the front porch so we could sleep under the stars like I did when I was a child. It felt comforting to stare into the familiar, awe-inspiring cosmos knowing that I would still have this reminder of wonder when I woke up the next day.

Greta was gone or integrated; my superpowers were faded; there was barely a trick of the light, and tiredness was finally coming to my body. I knew that sometime soon, I would fall asleep and leave this realm, possibly for the rest of this life. Part of me might be dying when I close my eyes to sleep. As buddy fell into slumber, I felt full emotions of love for my new self, a little bit of distant fear, and a whole lot of curiosity. Mostly though, I felt acceptance and trust that if I fell asleep in this world and woke in a different one entirely, I would be ok. This soul's consciousness I was experiencing would exist and has probably always existed. I just lay there feeling connected to it all.

Sometime in the wee hours of the morning on that starry, moonless night, I decided to close my eyes and relax my body. I watched my breath like the tide on the ocean without trying to change it — what a juxtaposition from when I came into this trip. Gently I slipped into sleep without noticing...

17
And She Lived Happily - enough After...

My life is not perfect, nor will it ever be. I've never had any delusion that life was anything more than one challenge after the next. It's just that now, I get to decide how I want to handle it. I still get upset and wonder if I'm acting like a lunatic now and again. I just look back at old journal entries and remember that I'm not that upset.

I see the negative self-beliefs and work to replace them with a more balanced view. I try to meditate every day and make that goal often enough to profess a daily meditation practice.

So what about the suicidal thoughts? Well, for the first couple of months post-Iboga, I was hopeful that the thoughts were just gone. That's what infinite Love can get you. Truthfully, they are not entirely gone, but when they do surface, they are simply thoughts. They are remnants of old neurological pathways with no emotional suffering attached, wispy and paper thin, easily blown away with a mindful breath. Now I see them for what they are, a cry of deeper distress, actionable and useful.

I'm still in psycho-educational classes online and seek every opportunity for learning new skills. I no longer let my rational mind limit the usefulness of any opportunity in acquiring skills or experience flow states from novelty whether it be trying new psychology or sound healing.

I journal all my bothersome thoughts to slow the rumination. I ask powerful questions! I clarify what people mean when emotions flare. And I sit in uncomfortable emotions without mentally or physically running away. It takes work but is still easier than tormenting myself the way I had in the past.

Integration is a daily thing for all of us. We live and experience only to turn around and contemplate what it all means. Sharing our pain and happiness, and feeling connectedness is the quintessential experience of being human.

Jamie Wheal talks about the flow cycle being: struggle, release, flow, and recovery. I would add integration to the end of the cycle. Integration is the moment when we are receptive to seeing the pattern of our existence and hold the effable and ineffable in the same breath.

'Life is a series of choices with unknown outcomes.'
~E.J.O.

Appendix A

Postscript- Letters to different audience members

Dear Trauma Sufferer,
This is not "the way." It was my way, and I'm hopeful that it will help to illuminate your own path. Life is like a video game: Gather your team of freaks around you for support. Ask experts how to find the cheat codes. Remember that leveling up may require challenging the same Boss several times. There is always a new next level with new challenges. Most importantly, you are the hero of your story.

To my 6 grade English Teacher,
Thank you more than words can tell. You gave me writing and so I'm writing my own happy ending.

To Academia and Medical Professionals,
I believe in a biopsychosociospiritual model of human development. In other words, all the answers are the answers. We have spent years isolating compounds and variables in science, and it's time we begin re-assembling them into working models of change. It's time to allow the clients to choose the modes of

recovery in whichever order they choose with a plan to introduce all the possible modalities for complete healing.

Additionally, I am a highly motivated clinician looking for connections and opportunities for further learning. Please feel free to contact me with any professional inquiries into my work. I am a case study of one and offer an exceptional interaction with professionals by being a clinician and a patient at the same time. I'm also looking to work toward my master's degree in adjacent topics to my own journey. Please contact me if you need a research assistant with my experience.
Altered.States.Integration@gmail.com

To Greta,
Thanks for secretly taking care of me for all those hard years. You loved me when I didn't know how.

Sincerely,
~e.j.o.

Printed in Poland
by Amazon Fulfillment
Poland Sp. z o.o., Wrocław

31251655R00036